I0820451
WORLD'S
SCARIEST
CREATURES
BY JOHN LESLEY
NASTY
STINGERS
Gareth Stevens
PUBLISHING

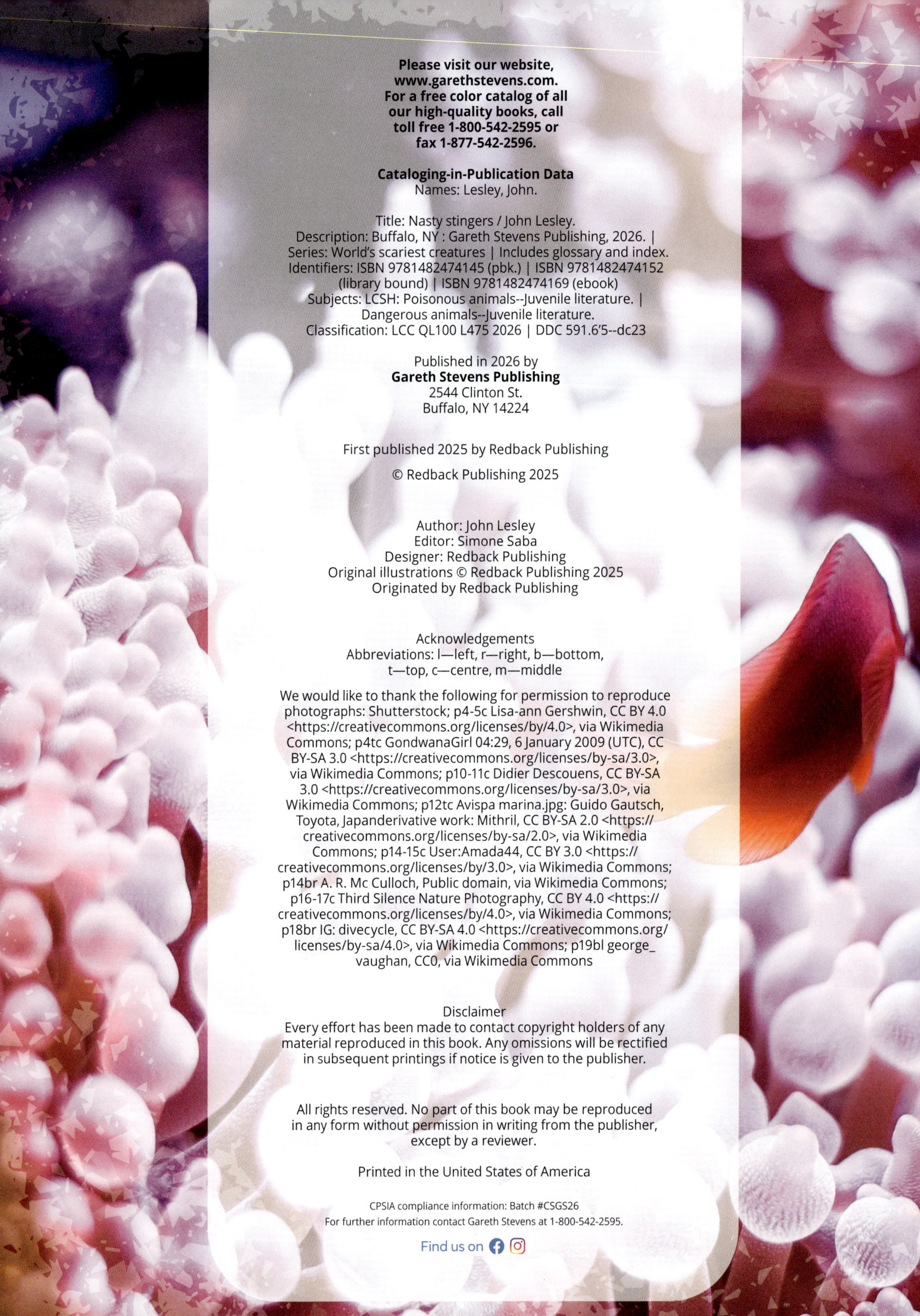

Please visit our website,
www.garethstevens.com.
For a free color catalog of all
our high-quality books, call
toll free 1-800-542-2595 or
fax 1-877-542-2596.

Cataloging-in-Publication Data
Names: Lesley, John.

Title: Nasty stingers / John Lesley.
Description: Buffalo, NY : Gareth Stevens Publishing, 2026. | Series: World's scariest creatures | Includes glossary and index.
Identifiers: ISBN 9781482474145 (pbk.) | ISBN 9781482474152 (library bound) | ISBN 9781482474169 (ebook)
Subjects: LCSH: Poisonous animals--Juvenile literature. | Dangerous animals--Juvenile literature.
Classification: LCC QL100 L475 2026 | DDC 591.6'5--dc23

Published in 2026 by
Gareth Stevens Publishing
2544 Clinton St.
Buffalo, NY 14224

First published 2025 by Redback Publishing

Author: John Lesley
Editor: Simone Saba
Designer: Redback Publishing
Original illustrations © Redback Publishing 2025
Originated by Redback Publishing

Acknowledgements
Abbreviations: l—left, r—right, b—bottom, t—top, c—centre, m—middle

We would like to thank the following for permission to reproduce photographs: Shutterstock; p4-5c Lisa-ann Gershwin, CC BY 4.0 <https://creativecommons.org/licenses/by/4.0>, via Wikimedia Commons; p4tc GondwanaGirl 04:29, 6 January 2009 (UTC), CC BY-SA 3.0 <https://creativecommons.org/licenses/by-sa/3.0>, via Wikimedia Commons; p10-11c Didier Descouens, CC BY-SA 3.0 <https://creativecommons.org/licenses/by-sa/3.0>, via Wikimedia Commons; p12tc Avispa marina.jpg: Guido Gautsch, Toyota, Japanderivative work: Mithril, CC BY-SA 2.0 <https://creativecommons.org/licenses/by-sa/2.0>, via Wikimedia Commons; p14-15c User:Amada44, CC BY 3.0 <https://creativecommons.org/licenses/by/3.0>, via Wikimedia Commons; p14br A. R. Mc Culloch, Public domain, via Wikimedia Commons; p16-17c Third Silence Nature Photography, CC BY 4.0 <https://creativecommons.org/licenses/by/4.0>, via Wikimedia Commons; p18br IG: divecycle, CC BY-SA 4.0 <https://creativecommons.org/licenses/by-sa/4.0>, via Wikimedia Commons; p19bl george_vaughan, CC0, via Wikimedia Commons

Printed in the United States of America

CPSIA compliance information: Batch #CSGS26
For further information contact Gareth Stevens at 1-800-542-2595.

Find us on

CONTENTS

Irukandji Jellyfish 4
Blue-Ringed Octopus 6
Bluebottle 8
Cone Snail 10
Box Jellyfish 12
Short-Tail Stingray 14
Puffer fish 16
Sea Snakes 18
Stonefish 20
Sea Anemone 22
Sponges 24
Stingers Around the World 26
How Dangerous Are They? 28
Safety in the Ocean 30
Glossary (Stinger Word List) 31
Index 32

IRUKANDJI JELLYFISH

Carukia barnesi

IRUKANDJI JELLYFISH

This tiny jellyfish packs a punch! At only 0.8 inch (2 cm) wide and see-through, Irukandji jellyfish are easy to miss if you are swimming, snorkeling, or diving nearby. Their four stinging tentacles are almost invisible and can trail for up to 20 inches (50 cm) in the water.

WHAT HAPPENS IF YOU ARE STUNG?

Irukandji toxin affects the brain and nervous system. Some people can get very sick, and the toxin can be fatal. Intense pain, nausea, and difficulty breathing are common. This may occur within the first hour after being stung.

An Irukandji jellyfish stings by shooting poisoned arrows or barbs that are stored in tiny capsule-like cells called nematocysts. Once triggered by motion sensors, this tiny-arrow attack allows the Irukandji to quickly catch and immobilize prey. It then draws this fresh meal up into its mouth using its tentacles.

FACT

There's a good reason Irukandjis are also called "stingers"!

FACT FILE

Length: bell is about 0.8 inch (2 cm) wide
Tentacles: 4 tentacles up to 20 inches (50 cm) long
Color: translucent
Poisonous: yes
Habitat: warm oceans
Scientific name: *Carukia barnesi*

FACT

The experts say you will feel a sense of "impending doom" after being stung by an Irukandji. This condition is called Irukandji syndrome.

AVOID BEING A VICTIM

1. Wear a full body suit.
2. Seek advice from experts.
3. Swim at beaches patrolled by lifeguards.
4. Don't touch an Irukandji. Even if it is dead on the beach, it can still sting.

WHERE DO THEY LIVE?

Irukandji live in the ocean in warm and temperate regions around the world.

BLUE-RINGED OCTOPUS

Hapalochlaena

The little blue-ringed octopus is a plain brown or sandy color until it gets upset. Then bright blue circles appear all over its body. This is its warning signal to get back or it will bite.

BITE

The bite itself causes little pain, and some people do not realize they have been bitten until they start to feel very sick. This is the stage at which the octopus venom is starting to take effect and medical help is needed urgently.

VENOM

The octopus uses its venom to immobilize its food so that it can eat without the little fish or crustacean escaping. The venom is also useful for fighting off predators such as sharks and humans.

HUMAN CONTACT

Humans usually encounter a blue-ringed octopus when investigating rock pools, or when diving. The octopus can squeeze itself into a discarded shell or even a piece of human garbage like a drink can.

FACT

Octopuses have good eyesight, so they can see you coming!

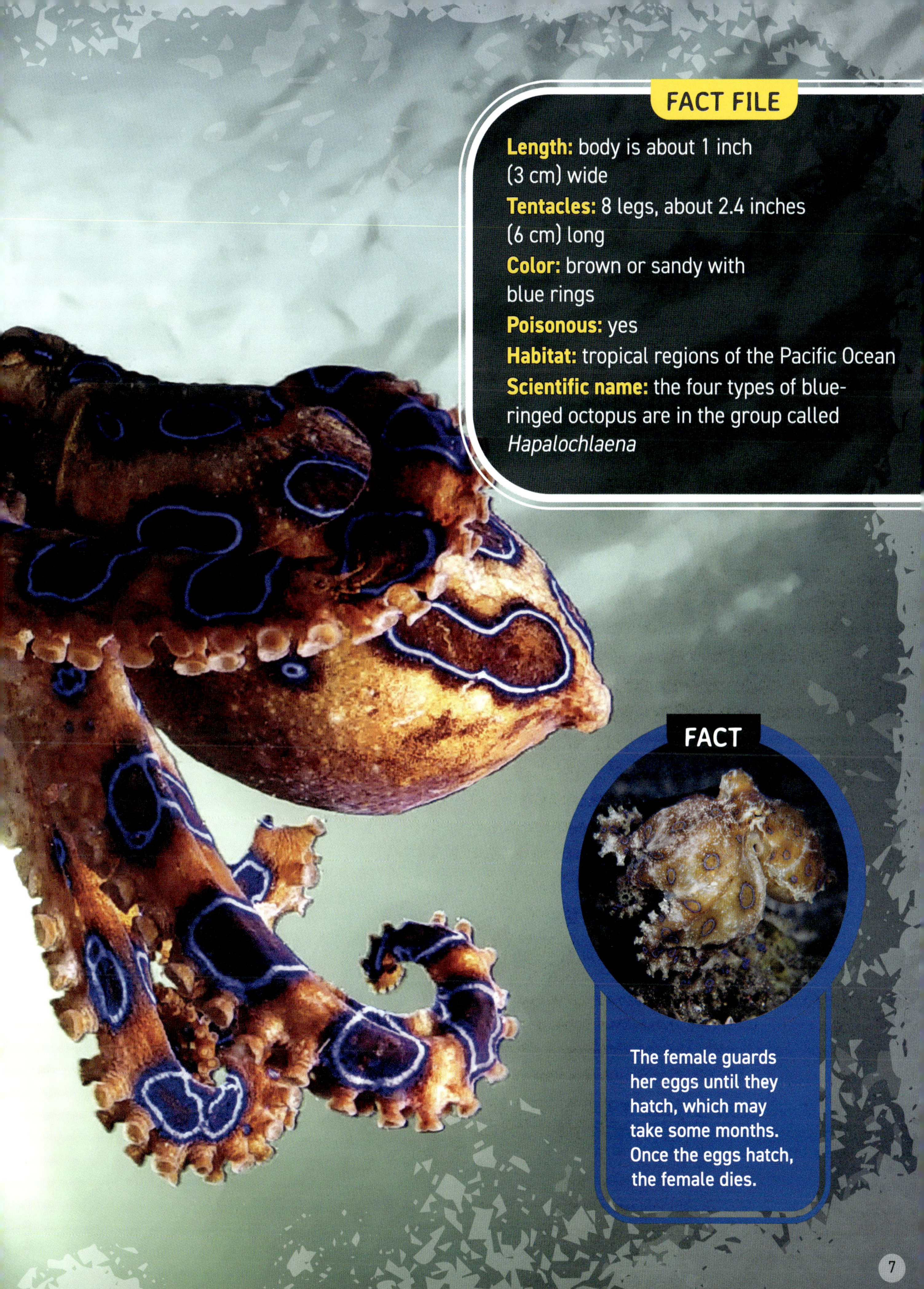

FACT FILE

Length: body is about 1 inch (3 cm) wide

Tentacles: 8 legs, about 2.4 inches (6 cm) long

Color: brown or sandy with blue rings

Poisonous: yes

Habitat: tropical regions of the Pacific Ocean

Scientific name: the four types of blue-ringed octopus are in the group called *Hapalochlaena*

FACT

The female guards her eggs until they hatch, which may take some months. Once the eggs hatch, the female dies.

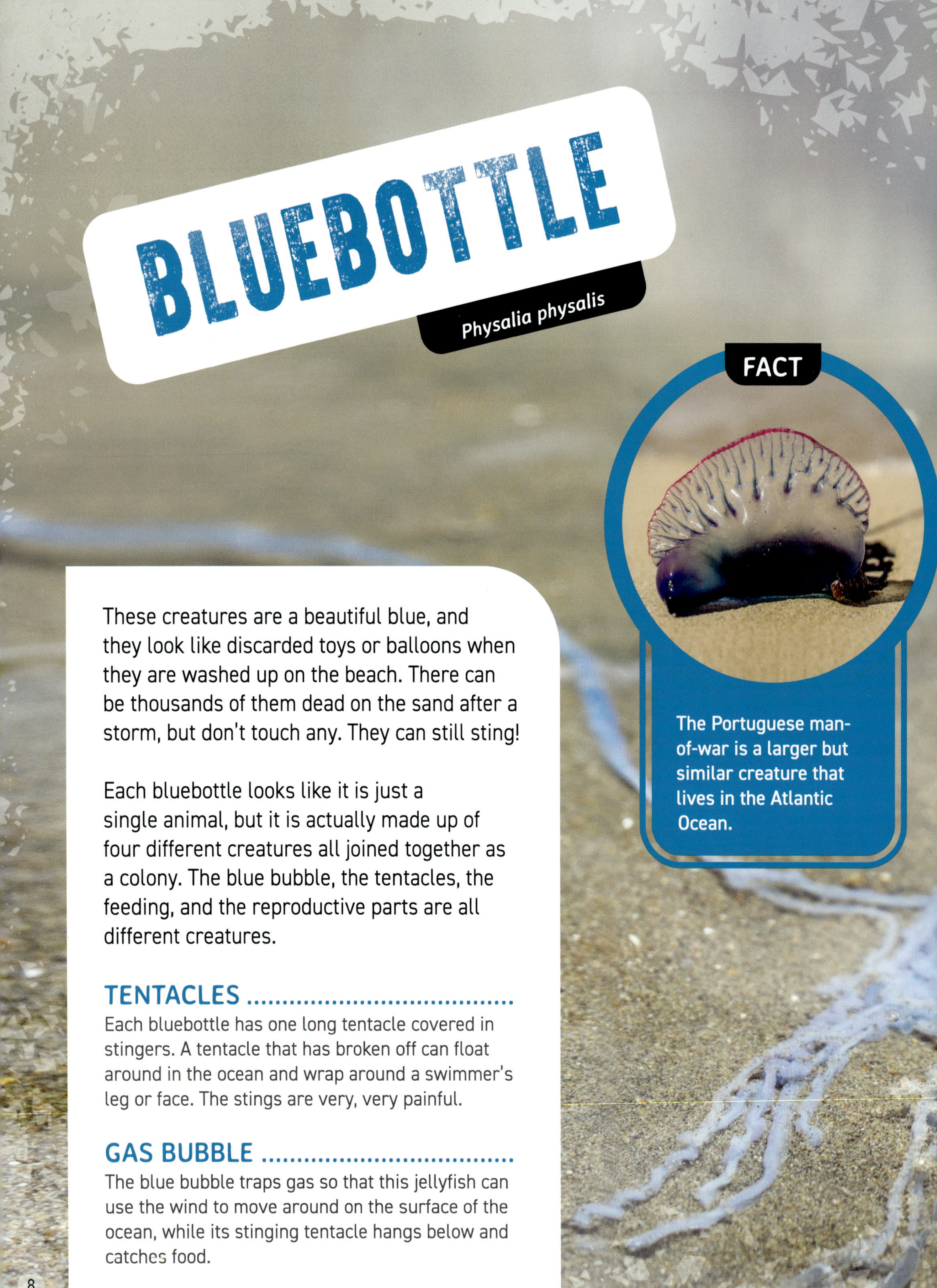

BLUEBOTTLE

Physalia physalis

These creatures are a beautiful blue, and they look like discarded toys or balloons when they are washed up on the beach. There can be thousands of them dead on the sand after a storm, but don't touch any. They can still sting!

Each bluebottle looks like it is just a single animal, but it is actually made up of four different creatures all joined together as a colony. The blue bubble, the tentacles, the feeding, and the reproductive parts are all different creatures.

TENTACLES

Each bluebottle has one long tentacle covered in stingers. A tentacle that has broken off can float around in the ocean and wrap around a swimmer's leg or face. The stings are very, very painful.

GAS BUBBLE

The blue bubble traps gas so that this jellyfish can use the wind to move around on the surface of the ocean, while its stinging tentacle hangs below and catches food.

FACT

The Portuguese man-of-war is a larger but similar creature that lives in the Atlantic Ocean.

FACT

Warning signs are often displayed on patrolled beaches if bluebottles are around.

FACT FILE

Length: body is 1.2 to 2 inches (3 to 5 cm)

Tentacles: can grow to 10 feet (3 m) long

Color: blue

Stingers: yes

Habitat: warm ocean water in the Pacific and Indian Oceans

Scientific name: *Physalia physalis*

Bluebottles are related to corals.

CONE SNAIL

Conus geographus

The cone snail has a beautiful shell, but inside it lives a highly poisonous mollusk. There are hundreds of different types of cone snails. One of the most dangerous ones is *Conus geographus*.

POISON DARTS

Being a mollusk, the cone snail cannot move quickly to hunt fish to eat, but the development of its toxic venom makes up for the snail's slowness. The snail hunts by shooting poisonous darts at its prey or any human who gets too close. A poisoned fish will stop moving so that the snail can eat it, and a human can die from the effects of the poison.

FACT

Scientists are researching whether a cone snail's deadly venom could be turned into a life-saving medicine.

FACT FILE

Length: shell up to 5.5 inches (15 cm) long, but the foot of the mollusk can extend out much further

Color: purple and brown patterns on the shell and body

Poison: lethal to humans

Habitat: oceans and seas, tropical parts of the Indian and Pacific Oceans

Scientific name: *Conus geographus*

FACT

Shell collectors all want at least one cone shell in their collection, but you should never pick up a live cone shell from the ocean. They are all dangerous.

BOX JELLYFISH

Chironex fleckeri

The box jellyfish is one of the most dangerous creatures in the ocean. They live in shallow coastal waters of the Indo-Pacific region, including northern Australia, Southeast Asia, and parts of the Indian Ocean. They are also found in warm seas in many other parts of the world.

TENTACLES

They look like a translucent, white box, with stinging tentacles dangling 9.8 feet (3 m) down from each corner. However, if you see a box jellyfish that does not seem to have tentacles, don't be fooled! They can also contract their tentacles into bundles only as big as a fist.

VENOM

The venom of box jellyfish is very strong and can cause extreme pain, cardiovascular collapse, and even death in humans.

DIET

The box jellyfish uses its stinging tentacles to catch its food, which includes prawns and small fish.

FACT

The box jellyfish sting is more painful than that of an Irukandji.

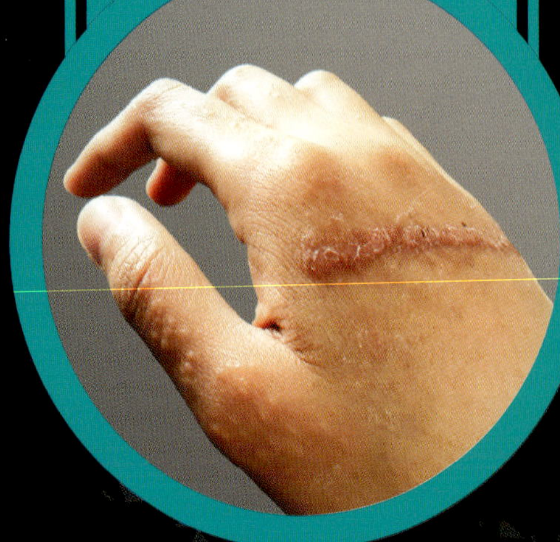

FACT FILE

Length: body is about 15.7 inches (40 cm) wide, tentacles are 10 feet (3 m) long

Tentacles: many tentacles with millions of stinging cells

Color: translucent white

Poisonous: stings can be fatal to humans

Habitat: warm ocean waters

Scientific name: *Chironex fleckeri*

FACT

The box jellyfish is also called a sea wasp. Its tentacles leave a long line of stings across a person's skin.

SHORT-TAIL STINGRAY

Dasyatis brevicaudata

FACT

The cartilage of stingrays is the same type of tissue that humans have in the flexible parts of their ears and nose.

FACT

Famous naturalist, Steve Irwin, died in 2006 after he was pierced by a stingray barb.

The stingray glides through the ocean, using its delta-shaped flippers like wings. There are many different species, ranging in size from 1 to 6.5 feet (0.30 to 2 m) wide. They are related to sharks and are cartilaginous fish, which means they do not have hard bones, but instead support their bodies internally with soft cartilage.

WEAPON

The short-tail stingray has stingers and a sharp spike on its long tail. They use their tail as a weapon when they feel threatened.

FACT FILE

Length: up to 6.5 feet (2 m) wide and 13 feet (4 m) long including the tail

Tail: double tail with barbs and a venomous, dagger-like spike up to 1 foot (30 cm) long

Color: gray and white

Poisonous: stings and piercing can be fatal to humans

Scientific name: *Dasyatis brevicaudata*

Other name: Smooth stingray

PUFFER FISH

Tetractenos

FACT

In Japan, poisonous puffer fish are prepared by special chefs who know which parts can be eaten. This dangerous meal is called *fugu*.

There are over 120 species of puffer fish, each with unique characteristics and adaptations to their environments. Many puffer fish contain tetrodotoxin, a potent neurotoxin that is extremely toxic, more poisonous than cyanide, and can be lethal to predators and humans if ingested.

When threatened, puffer fish inflate their bodies by ingesting water or air, making them appear much larger and more difficult for a predator to swallow. Some species also have spines that stick out when inflated.

FACT FILE

Length: ranges from a few inches to over 2 feet (0.6 m) in length

Color: various colors and patterns

Poisonous: yes

Habitat: coral reefs, coastal areas, lagoons, and estuaries

FACT

When threatened, they puff up their body to appear bigger by swallowing water or air.

SEA SNAKES

YELLOW-BELLIED SEA SNAKE

Sea snakes have evolved to live in the water, but they still need to come to the surface to breathe air.

Some sea snakes look like eels, but you can tell that you have seen a snake if it does not have a fin along its back. Only eels have a dorsal fin. Sea snakes have strong venom and if they feel threatened they can attack people in the water. People fishing with nets are at most risk of a bite from a sea snake if they catch one in their nets.

FACT

Sea snakes need strong venom so they can quickly immobilize a fish and swallow it before it swims away!

FACT

Sea snakes evolved from land-living snakes, but now they cannot survive long on land.

STONEFISH

Synanceia

Synanceia horrida

Stonefish are considered the most venomous fish in the world. Their sting can be fatal to humans. Along its back, the stonefish has spines attached to venom sacs.

They look like stones or pieces of coral and they sit motionless on the sea floor, sometimes covered in sand. Swimmers who touch one can suffer immediate, intense pain and quickly develop breathing difficulties.

FACT

Stonefish spines are only used against predators, and not for catching food.

FACT FILE

Length: 12 inches (30 cm) long
Color: mottled brown, gray, and red
Poisonous: yes
Habitat: shallow oceans, rock pools, and river mouths in warm oceans
Scientific names:
Synanceia verrucosa
Synanceia horrida

FACT

Stonefish will not swim away if touched and will depend on their poison for protection.

SEA ANEMONE

Beautiful sea anemones are related to jellyfish, but they attach themselves to surfaces rather than swimming in the ocean. Anemones have many different shapes, sizes, and colors, and they make up a large part of coral reef life.

Anemones have tentacles that can be pulled back into the body for protection. The tentacles have stinging cells that shoot out venom in a tiny spear that can both catch prey and also deter predators.

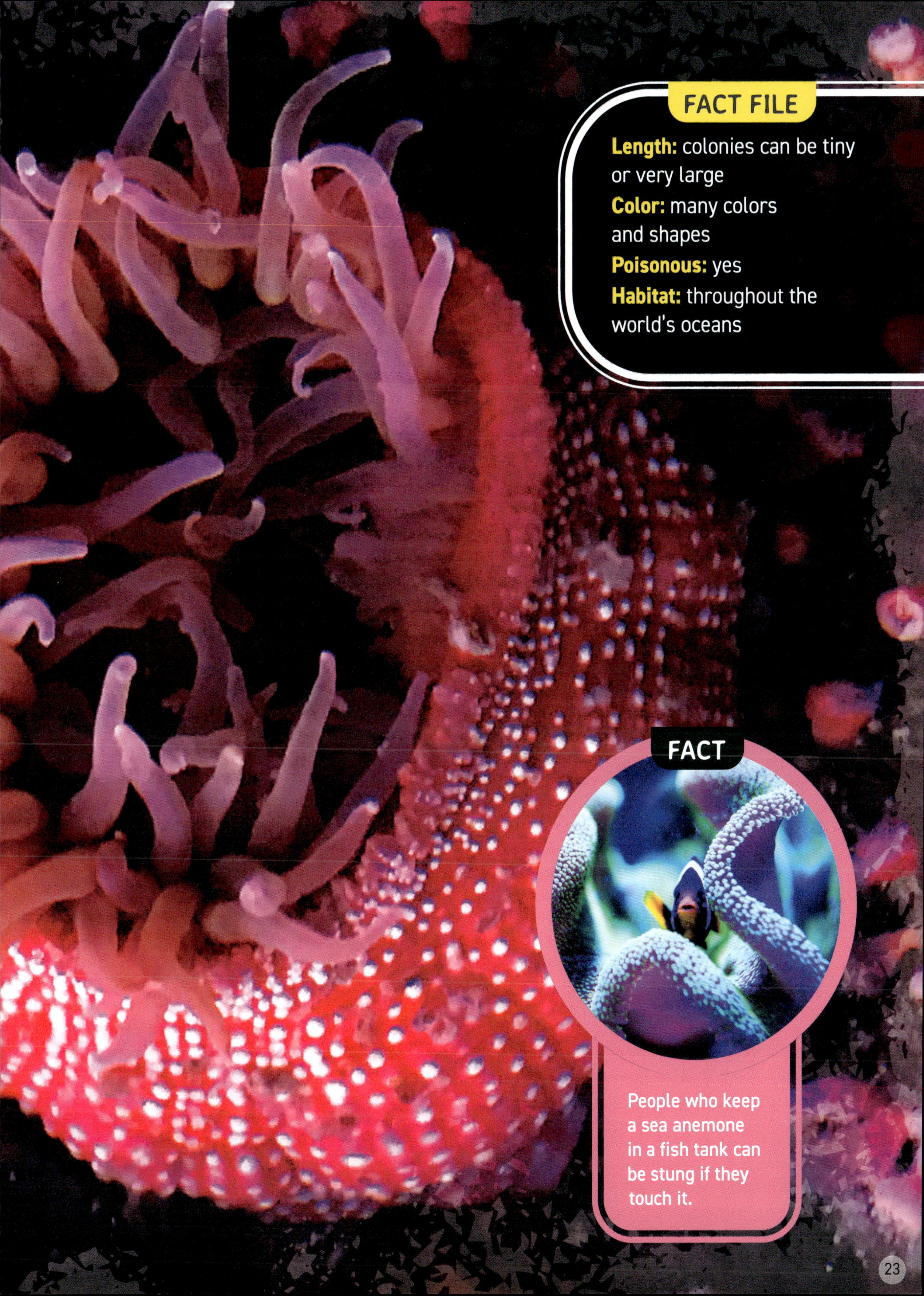

FACT FILE

Length: colonies can be tiny or very large

Color: many colors and shapes

Poisonous: yes

Habitat: throughout the world's oceans

FACT

People who keep a sea anemone in a fish tank can be stung if they touch it.

SPONGES

FACT

Natural sponges can be used to wash with in the bath. These are the soft skeletons of sea sponges and do not have sharp spikes.

The sponge is a very ancient type of aquatic animal in a group called *Porifera*. They may look like a rock or even a plant and are covered in small holes, which they use to filter their food out of the ocean water. A piece cut off from a living sponge can grow into a whole new animal.

Touching some sponges (in particular the bright red fire sponges), can cause a painful rash on human skin.

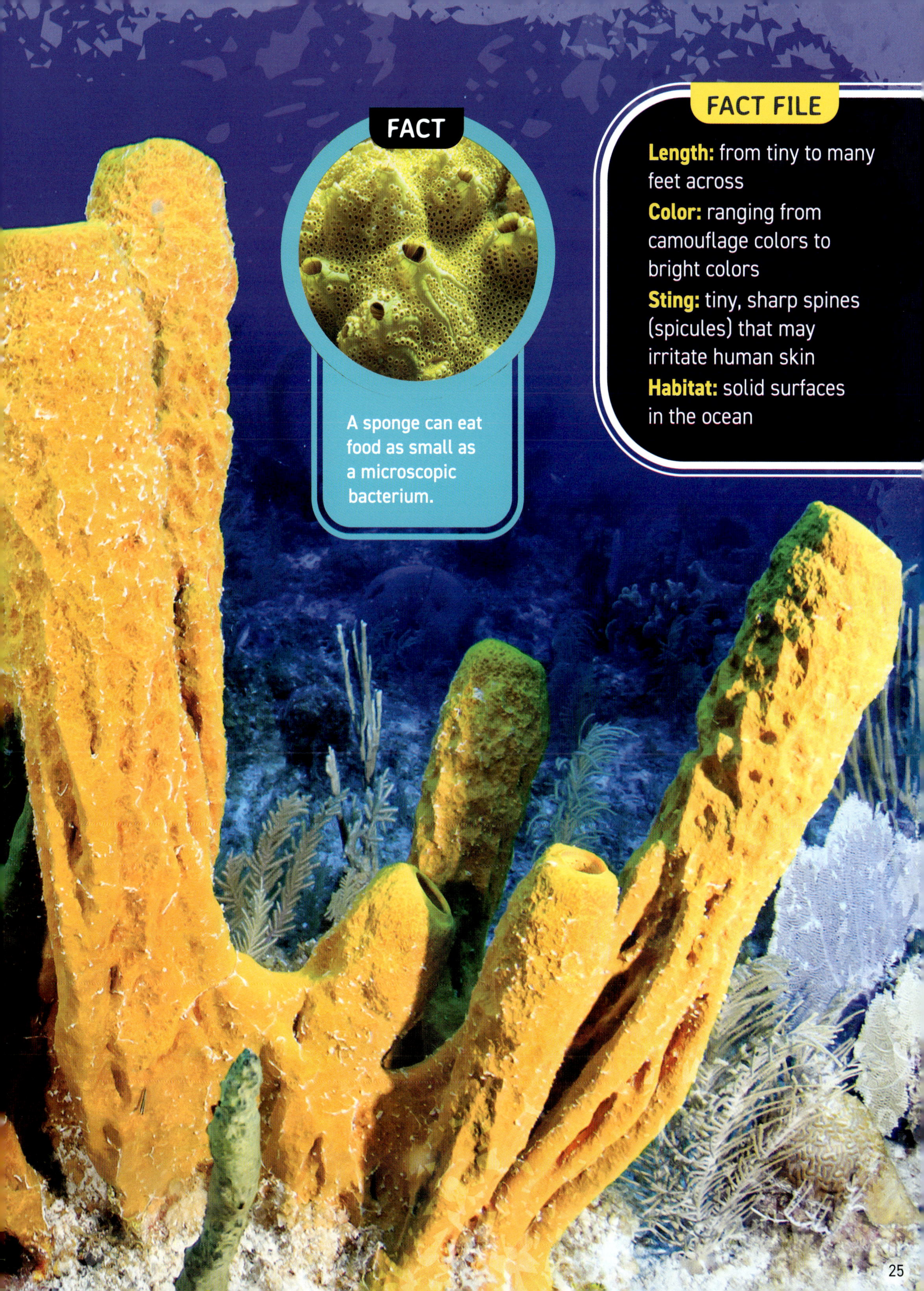

FACT

A sponge can eat food as small as a microscopic bacterium.

FACT FILE

Length: from tiny to many feet across

Color: ranging from camouflage colors to bright colors

Sting: tiny, sharp spines (spicules) that may irritate human skin

Habitat: solid surfaces in the ocean

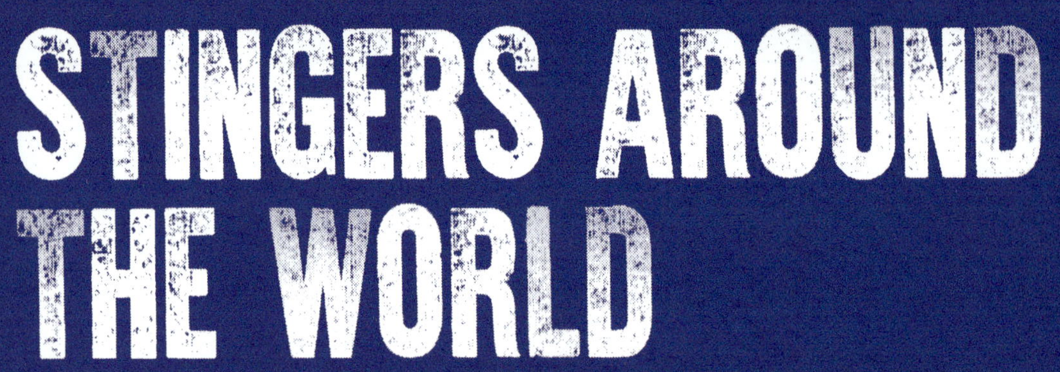

STINGERS AROUND THE WORLD

ELECTRIC EEL

These eels can produce enough electricity in their skin to give a human a nasty electric shock. They live in South America in the Amazon River region.

SCORPION FISH

These fish have venom-coated spines on their back. Despite this, the fish is often caught by fishers and prepared as a meal.

CATFISH

Catfish are often caught by people fishing. The sharp spines on catfish fins can cause painful stings.

SEA URCHIN

Sea urchins are collected for food by people around the world. Before the sea urchins can be eaten in a meal, the long, sharp spines that they use to protect themselves have to be removed. A spine can stick through a foot or hand, causing an extremely painful injury.

Hydroids are stinging animals that look like plants or feathers growing on top of coral or on rocks on the sea floor. Their bodies are covered in stinging cells.

HOW DANGEROUS ARE THEY?

Creatures in the sea that sting, bite, and inject poison have all evolved to have these adaptations for two main purposes. Firstly, they need to kill food, and secondly, they need to protect themselves from becoming food for a predator.

People who enjoy swimming and diving in the sea are likely to come into contact with poison from one of these creatures at some time. The results can range from mild and annoying to deadly.

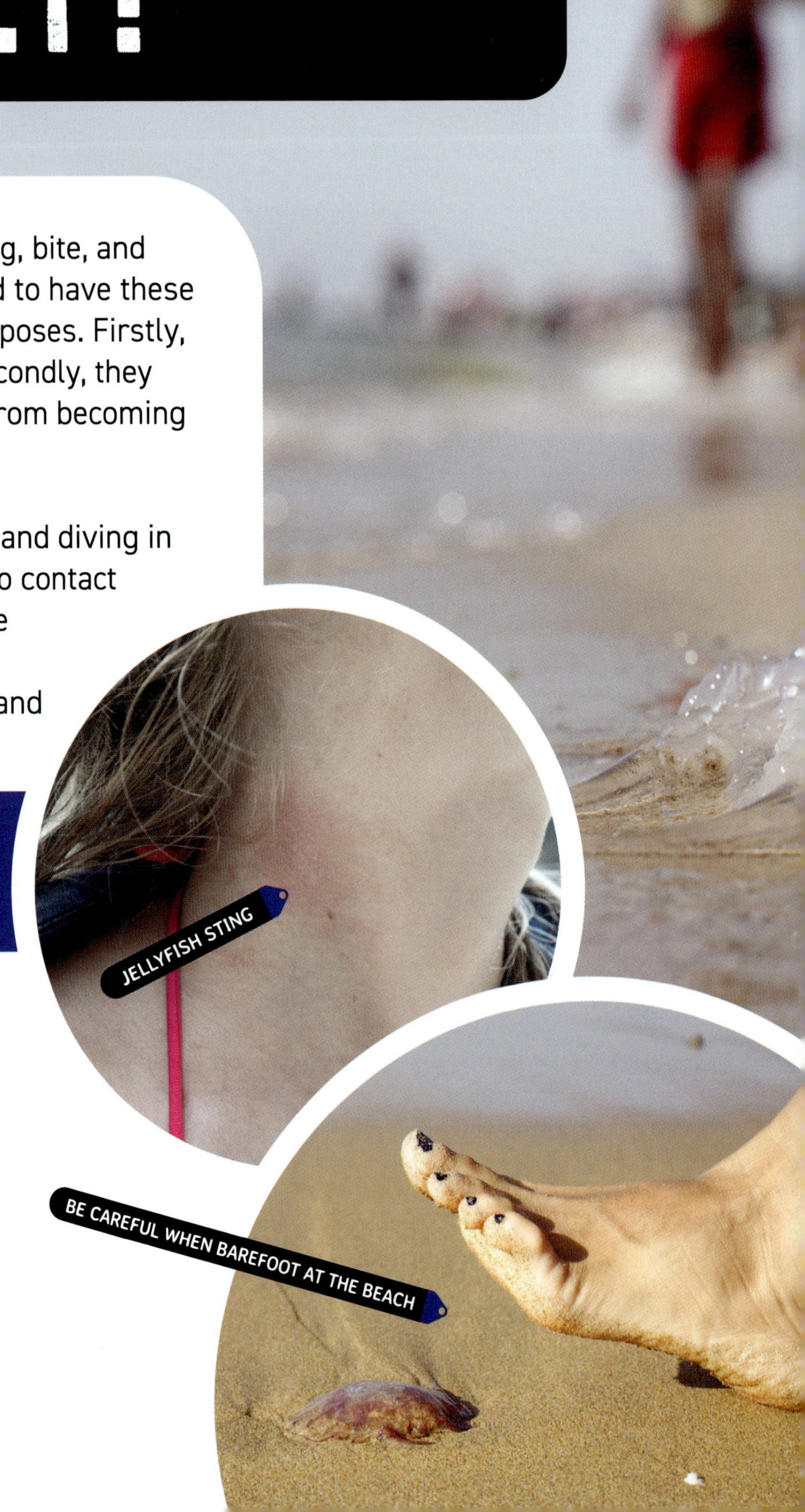

Here are some of the effects these poisons can have on humans:

- Pain at the site of the sting
- Muscle pain throughout the body
- Difficulty breathing
- Fever
- Vomiting
- Sweating
- Confusion
- Paralysis
- Fainting
- Death

BOX JELLYFISH STING INJURY

WARNING

Coastlines that have a lot of stingers will often display warning signs.

SAFETY IN THE OCEAN

Wear a wetsuit or clothing that covers the skin.

Wear goggles.

Swim at patrolled beaches where the lifeguards can help in the event of an emergency.

Be aware that you share the water with billions of other creatures.

GLOSSARY

Stinger Word List

cartilaginous made of soft cartilage

crustaceans prawns, crabs, lobsters

delta-shaped shaped like a letter D

mollusk animal group that includes snails, mussels, and octopuses

mottled mixed colors and patterns

nausea feeling like vomiting

nematocyst tiny capsule that holds stinging barbs

sac pouch or bag-like structure

sense of impending doom feeling that something very bad is about to happen

toxin poison

translucent letting some light through

venom poison that is injected

Keep yourself and your pets away from dead stinging animals on the beach.

Don't poke at creatures in rock pools or when diving or snorkeling.

INDEX

catfish 27
electric eel 26
fugu 16
hydroid 27
Irwin, Steve 14
pets 31
Porifera 24
Portuguese man-of-war 8
rock pools 6, 21, 31
scorpion fish 26
sea urchin 27
smooth stingray 15
spicule 25